CurriculumVisions

# The ancient Greeks

## SECOND EDITION

## Dr Brian Knapp

## ⚠ Look after our world heritage!

It is easy to talk about looking after the environment, but we each have to help. Help is often small things, like being careful when you walk around old buildings, and not leaving scratch marks on anything that you visit. It doesn't take a lot of effort – just attitude.

# ( Curriculum Visions )

## There's much more on-line including videos

You will find multimedia resources covering a wide range of topics in the Professional Zone at:

## ( www.CurriculumVisions.com )

A CVP Book
**This second edition © Earthscape 2009**

First edition 2006

**Author**
*Brian Knapp, BSc, PhD*

**Art Director**
*Duncan McCrae, BSc*

**Senior Designer**
*Adele Humphries, BA, PGCE*

**Editor**
*Lisa Magloff, MA, and Gillian Gatehouse*

**Designed and produced by**
*EARTHSCAPE*

**Printed in China by**
*WKT Company Ltd*

**The ancient Greeks 2nd Edition – Curriculum Visions
A CIP record for this book is
available from the British Library**

**Paperback ISBN 978 1 86214 601 3**

**Illustrations**
*Mark Stacey* (cover background, pages 2, 3b, 9, 12, 13, 14–15, 16, 17, 18–19, 20–21, 26, 27, 30–31, 32–33, 34, 35, 36–37, 38–39, 40, 42–43), *David Woodroffe* (pages 4, 6, 29, 30bl, 36tl, 37t, 39)

**Picture credits**
All photographs are from the Earthscape Picture Library except the following: *University of Pennsylvania Museum* pages 43, 44.

This product is manufactured from sustainable managed forests. For every tree cut down at least one more is planted.

*This book is dedicated to the memory
of Duncan McCrae 1965–2005.*

# Contents

▲ Helmet

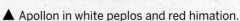

▲ Apollon in white peplos and red himation.

▲ Sound effects –
ancient Greek style.

# Who were the ancient Greeks?

**The ancient Greeks were peoples who lived from about 800 BC to 150 BC. They are famous for developing a way of living that we still use today.**

Modern Greece is a small mountainous country made up of a long finger of land (a **PENINSULA**) and hundreds of islands. It lies near the eastern end of the Mediterranean Sea.

## Many peoples

Ancient Greece was not a single country as we see it today (picture ①). Instead, it was a collection of peoples who shared the same language and history.

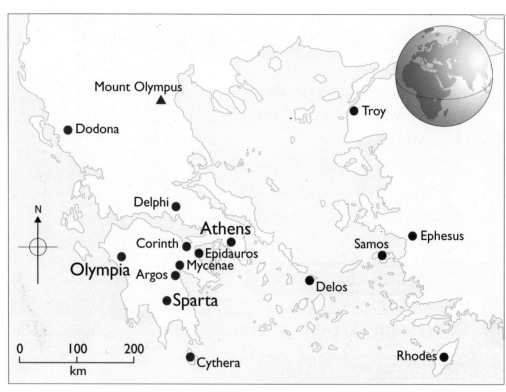

▲ ① Important sites from ancient Greece and the Greek colonies in ancient Persia (now Turkey).

## Early times

There was an ancient Greek civilisation in the **BRONZE AGE** – a time before the use of iron. The ancestors of the ancient Greeks lived in cities such as Troy (known for the legend of the Trojan Horse) and Mycenae (picture ②).

Their power faded away by about 1000 BC for reasons we do not know because their written language was lost. The time that followed this was called the **GREEK DARK AGES**, when people abandoned their cities.

## A land of cities

By about 800 BC the Greeks were once more building cities and they also began to write down their history. This is why many people choose this date as the start of ancient Greek times (picture ⑤).

Each group of people became based around a city in a valley, and was separated from its neighbours by tall ranges of mountains. As a result, the people would not have thought of themselves so much as 'Greeks', but as, for example, Athenians (those who belonged to the city of Athens) or Spartans (those who belonged to the city of Sparta), just as the Romans in later times were the people who came from the city of Rome, not Italy.

## Different ways of living

Each city developed its own ways of living. Cities were rivals and they often fought with one another (picture ③). They really only came together and made alliances when they were attacked by a neighbouring country such as Persia.

Only towards the end of Greek times would they have used the word **HELLENE**, which was their word for 'land of the Greeks'.

▲ ② This is the hilltop fort of King Agamemnon of Mycenae, one of the ancestors of the ancient Greeks.

▼ ③ Greek battle scene showing interlocking shields.

## Empire

The peoples from the ancient Greek cities captured parts of many neighbouring lands, and formed an empire whose people used the Greek language. For a short while, under the leadership of **ALEXANDER THE GREAT**, the empire swelled from lands along the coast of the Mediterranean Sea to include Egypt and also Asia as far as northern India. It was a huge empire for such a small country (picture ④).

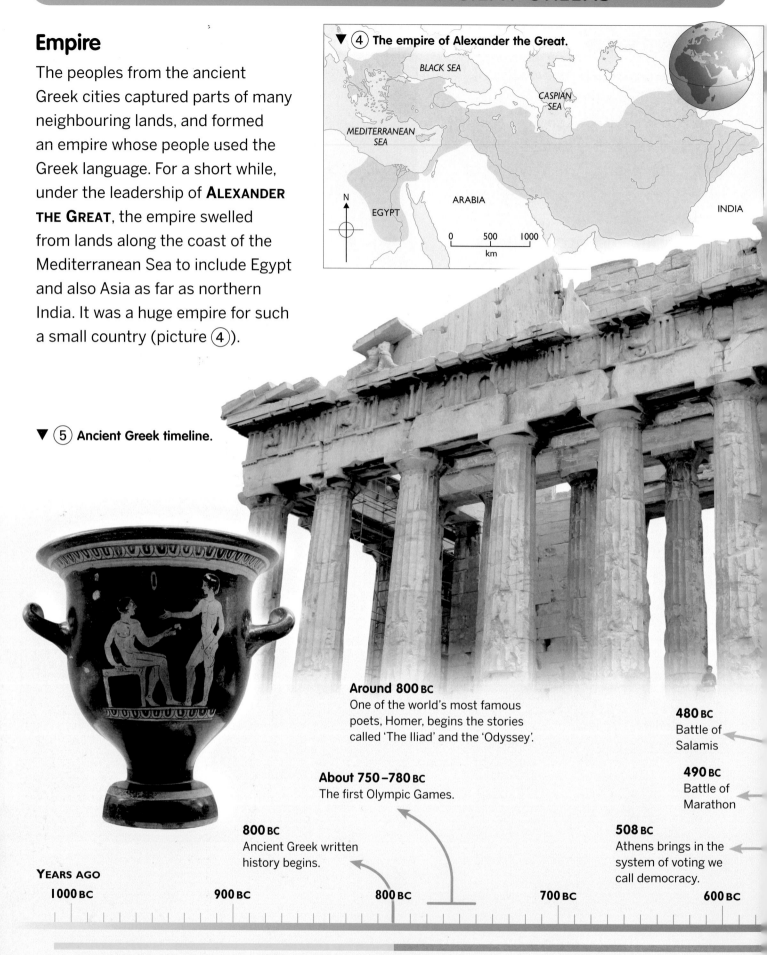

▼ ④ The empire of Alexander the Great.

BLACK SEA

CASPIAN SEA

MEDITERRANEAN SEA

EGYPT

ARABIA

INDIA

N

0    500    1000
km

▼ ⑤ Ancient Greek timeline.

**Around 800 BC**
One of the world's most famous poets, Homer, begins the stories called 'The Iliad' and the 'Odyssey'.

**480 BC**
Battle of Salamis

**About 750–780 BC**
The first Olympic Games.

**490 BC**
Battle of Marathon

**800 BC**
Ancient Greek written history begins.

**508 BC**
Athens brings in the system of voting we call democracy.

**YEARS AGO**

1000 BC          900 BC          800 BC          700 BC          600 BC

**1100–800 BC Prehistoric Greece (no written records)**

**800–500 BC ARCHAEN PERIOD**

▼ The Parthenon (which dates from the Classical Period) is one of the most famous buildings in the world. Much of its detail is now lost, but you can still see the pleasing proportions and the way the columns taper slightly towards the top. This gives the huge building a more graceful appearance (see also page 15).

▶ Amazing sculptures such as this 6 m high statue of the god Apollon, were made in the Classical Period.

## The end of ancient Greek times

The time of the ancient Greeks lasted for about 700 years. Building and the arts were most developed around the 5th century BC and ancient Greece was most powerful around the time of Alexander the Great, in about 330 BC.

But after Alexander, the power of the ancient Greeks gradually declined and the Greeks were finally defeated by the Romans, making Greece part of the Roman empire in about 146 BC.

**432 BC**
The Parthenon is completed.

**472–410 BC**
Greeks develop the theatre in Athens. Many of the most famous Greek plays were written during this time.

**431–404 BC**
The Peloponnesian War breaks out between Athens and Sparta.

**146 BC**
Greece becomes part of the Roman empire.

**450 BC**
Athens becomes the most powerful city.

**404 BC**
Sparta defeats Athens.

**338 BC**
Philip, king of Macedonia, takes control of Greece.

**336–323 BC**
Alexander the Great, son of Philip, conquers the Middle East, North Africa and Asia as far as northern India.

500 BC          400 BC          300 BC          200 BC          100 BC

**500–323 BC CLASSICAL PERIOD**          **323–146 BC HELLENISTIC PERIOD**

# Land of mountains and sun

**Greece is a small country, made up of a peninsula and many islands, towards the east of the Mediterranean Sea.**

We know Greece as a land of summer sun and holiday beaches. But the ancient Greeks saw it very differently. They had to live here, and they found it surprisingly difficult.

## Mountains

Greece is an almost entirely mountainous land (picture ①) with only small areas of lowlands.

The mountains make Greece a very beautiful country, but one in which people cannot easily make a living from farming, or keep in contact with one another.

It was the mountains that made ancient Greece into a land of separate cities, each developing its own customs and ideas and not inclined to join with others into a single kingdom.

▼ ① Mountains of the Pelops.

## Weather

Greece has scorchingly hot, dry, sunny summers. Rain falls only in winter. Wheat and many other food crops will not grow in much of Greece.

This restricts crops in many areas to grapes and olives (picture ②) and animals to sheep and goats. As only a certain amount of food could be obtained locally, the Greeks built boats and took to fishing and to trade. But it was always tempting for each city to want to take over the lands of another, or to spread out on to lands belonging to their neighbours. It was a recipe for war.

▲ ② Olive oil, made from the fruits of the olive tree, was used in salads and in cooking, just as today. But it was also used as the fuel for oil lamps.

Producing olive oil was hard work. The ripe olives had to be placed between two wooden or stone discs and weights placed on them to squeeze out the oil. The crushed oil ran out into jars. Large numbers of olives were needed to make quite small amounts of oil.

▲ The god Zeus with his thunderbolt.

▲ Athena fighting a giant.

▲ Hermes

# Gods

**The Greeks thought that the world around them was controlled by super-humans. The most important were the 12 Olympian gods.**

Like all other civilisations, the ancient Greeks wanted to know about creation and life after death. They believed that the world was formed and controlled by a range of gods, each of which was responsible for one aspect of the world.

## Creation

The ancient Greeks imagined the world began as a result of the god Chaos. Chaos was the dark, silent depths filled with formless matter from which all things came into existence. The Greeks knew it as the cosmos. Chaos generated the solid mass of Earth, from which arose the starry, cloud-filled Heaven.

Mother Earth (Gaea) bore a son, Uranus, without help. She and her son Uranus were the parents of the first creatures, the Titans. Uranus hated these monsters, and, even though they were his children, he locked them in a secret place in the earth. Gaea was enraged at this and arranged for their release. The Titans were then responsible for many of the natural disasters that occurred, such as volcanic eruptions and lightning flashes.

Eventually the Titans were overthrown by their own children, now known as the **OLYMPIANS**, led by Zeus. The Olympians were the gods the ancient Greeks worshipped.

# The 12 gods of Olympus: the Olympians

One of the 12 Titans was called Cronus. He and his sister-queen, Rhea, became the parents of the most important gods and goddesses, known as the Olympians. Cronus had been warned that he would be overthrown by one of his own children. To prevent this, he swallowed his first five children as soon as they were born. Rhea did not like this. She substituted a stone wrapped in swaddling clothes for their sixth child, Zeus. He was hidden and when he was older, he returned and forced Cronus to disgorge all the other children, who had grown inside him. Zeus and his brothers and sisters fought a war against Cronus and the other Titans. Zeus won, and the Titans were confined in the deepest part of the underworld.

Zeus became ruler and protector of the gods of Mount Olympus and of mortals.

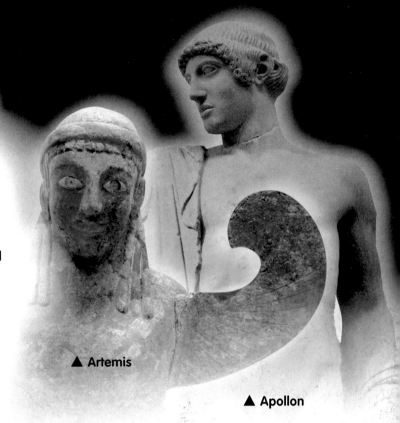

▲ Artemis

▲ Apollon

## Aphrodite
(Roman: Venus) The goddess of love and beauty. Symbols: sceptre, myrtle, dove.

Aphrodite loved and was loved by many gods and mortals. Among her mortal lovers, the most famous was perhaps Adonis.

## Apollon
(Roman: Apollo) God of the Sun, music and prophecy. Symbols: bow, lyre, laurel.

Apollon was an eternal youth who never became a man. He was a god of telling the future. He was also connected to medicine and healing. He was a master archer and a fleet-footed athlete, and was supposed to have been the first victor in the Olympic Games. He was famous for his oracle at Delphi. People travelled to it from all over the Greek world to try to learn about the future.

## Ares
(Roman: Mars) The god of war. Symbol: spear.

He was very aggressive. He was unpopular with both gods and humans. Ares was not invincible, even against mortals. He personified the brutal nature of war.

## Artemis
(Roman: Diana) The goddess of the hunt and the moon. Symbols: bow, deer.

## Athena
(Roman: Minerva) One of the most important goddesses. Goddess of wisdom, war, the arts, industry, justice, skill, farming and the patroness of Athens. Symbols: goatskin (shield), owl, olive tree.

Athena sprang full-grown and armoured from the forehead of the god Zeus and was his favourite child. She was fierce and brave in battle, but only fought to protect the state and home from outside enemies.

## Hades
(Roman: Pluto) Hades was the twelfth Olympian and god of the underworld, but he did not live on Mount Olympus. Hades, Poseidon and Zeus, drew lots for realms to rule. Zeus got the sky and earth, Poseidon got the seas, and Hades got the underworld, the unseen realm to which the dead go upon leaving the world.

## Hephaestus
(Roman: Vulcan) The god of fire and the forge. Symbol: axe.

## Hera
(Roman: Juno) The goddess of marriage. Symbols: ornamental staff, crown, peacock.

## Hermes
(Roman: Mercury) The god of travel and trade; messenger of the gods. Symbols: staff with two snakes wrapped around it, winged boots.

Hermes had winged sandals and a winged hat and bore a golden magic wand, wrapped around with snakes and wings. He led the souls of the dead to the underworld and was believed to possess magical powers over sleep and dreams.

## Hestia
(Roman: Vesta) The goddess of the hearth/family life. (Hestia eventually gave up her place to Dionysus).

## Poseidon
(Roman: Neptune) – god of the sea. Symbols: three-pronged spear, horse, bull.

His weapon was a trident, which could shake the earth, and shatter any object. He was second only to Zeus in power amongst the gods.

## Zeus
(Roman: Jupiter) God of the sky and earth; leader of the gods. Symbols: thunderbolt, eagle, oak.

# Sanctuaries and temples

**The ancient Greeks worshipped their gods in special areas called SANCTUARIES. Inside the sanctuaries were many TEMPLES.**

The ancient Greeks worshipped their gods by dedicating parts of the countryside to them. These sacred areas were called sanctuaries and they contained temples, **TREASURIES** and many other buildings. In Olympia, as in several other places, the sanctuary contained a sports stadium (see pages 40–45).

The main buildings were the temples (picture ②). They were rectangular and had gently sloping roofs. The Greeks, like the ancient Egyptians, did not know how to support a roof without using many columns. So they turned this limitation into a masterly piece of architecture.

▲ ① The ruins of the altar at the sanctuary of Apollon.

## The sanctuary at Delphi

Delphi is in the mountains north west of Athens. Here there was a sanctuary to the god Apollon (picture ①). It was believed that this sanctuary, built next to a sacred spring, marked the centre of the universe.

In the main temple to Apollon, an eternal flame burned. Legends tell of how Apollon first came to Delphi in the shape of a dolphin, carrying priests on his back.

Vapours seeped up into the temple through cracks in the floor. This may have put the future-teller, or oracle, into a trance and so allowed her to sing her prophesies. The vapours came from the earth goddess Gaea.

This oracle was extremely important to the ancient Greeks, and was consulted before all wars.

Important cities built treasuries at Delphi to thank the oracle for advice important to their victories. The largest is the Treasury of Athens, built to commemorate the Athenians' victory at the Battle of Marathon (see pages 36–37).

▶ The oracle at Delphi is said to have declared Socrates to be the wisest man in Greece, to which Socrates replied that if so, this was because he alone was aware of his own ignorance. This claim is related to one of the most famous mottos of Delphi, "know thyself".

## Temples

Inside the outer columns was the central sacred space, or **CELLA**. Inside the cella was an enormous statue of the god or goddess to whom the temple was dedicated.

Pilgrims brought gifts to the god or goddess, and when they had left these on a table in the cella, they would go out into the temple courtyard to a large outdoor altar and worship there. On special occasions, animals were brought as sacrifices to the gods and killed at the temple.

▼ ② **An ancient Greek temple.**

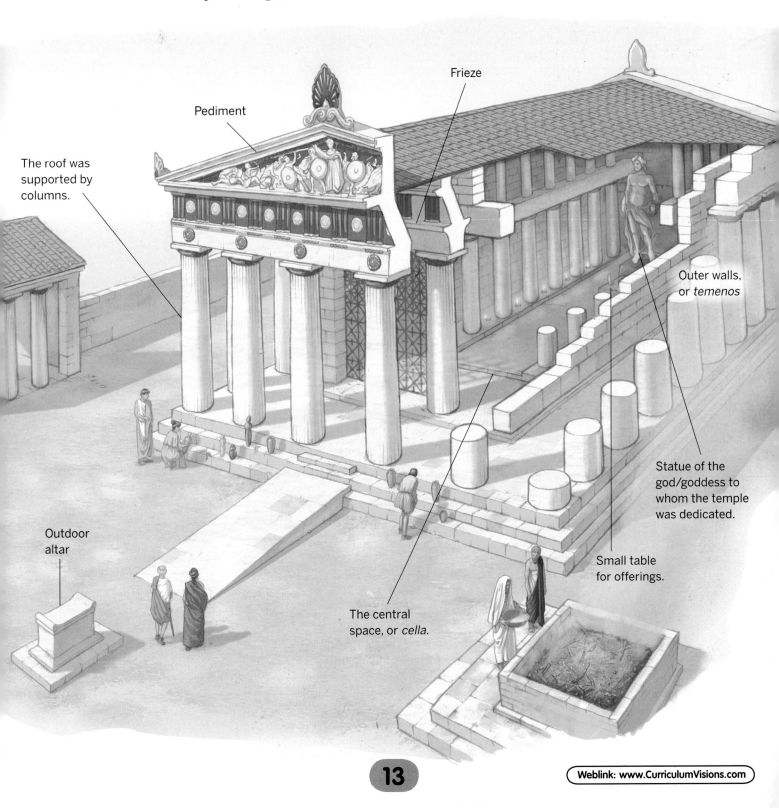

Pediment

Frieze

The roof was supported by columns.

Outer walls, or *temenos*

Statue of the god/goddess to whom the temple was dedicated.

Small table for offerings.

Outdoor altar

The central space, or *cella*.

## The Erechtheion

The Erechtheion was built in 420 BC. It has an IONIC style and is made of several separate parts, one part is dedicated to the goddess Athena, another part to the god Poseidon. It has an outside porch whose roof is supported by carved pillars, called the Caryatids, who are the maidens you can see here.

Erechtheion

Parthenon

Statue of Athena

Gatehouse

Enclosing wall

Athena Nike

## The Temple of Athena Nike

A Nike is a winged victory figure. This is the smallest of the temples, with just a row of four columns in front of each of its narrow sides. It was built next to the gatehouse to help protect the sanctuary area.

## The Parthenon

The Parthenon was built between 447 BC and 438 BC and the sculptures around the roof line (the frieze) were finished in 432 BC in honour of Athena, the goddess that looked after Athens.

The sculptures show the birth of Athena and the fight for the right to look after the city of Athens.

Inside the Parthenon, there was a statue of Athena over 10 metres high, made of pure ivory and gold.

The Parthenon was blown apart by a war between the Turks and the Venetians in 1687 and its central room, the *cella*, no longer exists. Nevertheless, the parts that remain show it to be one of the most beautiful buildings ever made.

Theatre

## The golden rectangle

A golden rectangle has sides in the proportions 16 to 10. Pythagoras, the ancient Greek mathematician, is thought to have discovered the shape of the golden rectangle. Many ancient buildings (including the Parthenon) have proportions similar to golden rectangles.

## The Acropolis of Athens

The most famous sanctuary from ancient Greek times is the Acropolis at Athens. It is an area of white limestone rock that was turned into a sanctuary enclosed and protected by a wall. The way in was through a massive gatehouse. Inside the sanctuary three principle temples were built. The greatest of these is one of the world's most instantly recognisable buildings: the Parthenon.

# Daily life in ancient Greece

**Ancient Greece was made up of a few wealthy people, free citizens and many slaves. Most lived in the countryside. Only the wealthy lived in the city.**

Life in ancient Greece, as in all other countries of the time, was based on wealth and power. Daily life for the wealthy and citizens depended on the house chores, the farming and the mining being done by slaves.

## Homes

Greece is hot and sunny in summer. In spring, autumn and winter a strong, chill wind can blow. As a result, homes (picture ①) were built around courtyards. The courtyard

▶ ② **An oil lamp.**

gave privacy, it gave shade from the sun and it gave protection from winter rain and wind. The courtyard was also the place where the whole family could sit in the evening by the light of oil lamps (picture ②) and listen to stories called **MYTHS** and **FABLES** (see pages 22–23).

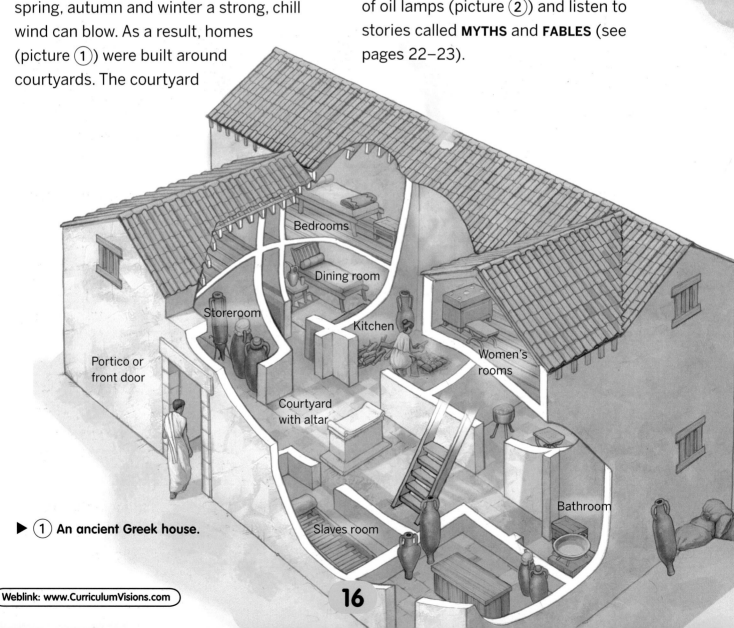

Bedrooms

Dining room

Storeroom

Kitchen

Women's rooms

Portico or front door

Courtyard with altar

Bathroom

Slaves room

▶ ① **An ancient Greek house.**

▲ ③ The AGORA, or marketplace.

Most houses were built on just one floor, although some had two storeys. Generally, houses had flat roofs covered with tiles or thatch, and walls made of mud bricks. This is why few of them survive.

The biggest and wealthiest homes had separate areas for women and men, and for cooking and bathing.

The home was the centre of life for Greek women as they were only rarely allowed to go out of the home. Beyond the walls it was a man's world – including the shopping (picture ③).

## Eating

In ancient Greek times, meat was a rare luxury and so most food was made of vegetables and cereals cooked in olive oil (see page 9). Goat and sheep milk was also made into feta-style cheese.

Bread was eaten where wheat was available (or for those who could pay for the wheat imported from Egypt and the Black Sea) and those near the sea had fish, such as anchovies and sardines.

Of course, fresh food was only available in summer, so the surplus had to be dried and stored to last through the winter when dried fish, pickled olives and cheese were eaten, along with dried beans. Grapes were dried to make raisins.

Drinking water was unclean in the cities and so most people drank very weak wine or beer (the alcohol in it kills the germs).

## Clothes and cleanliness

Remember that summers were hot, but winters cool or cold. So in summer it made sense to wear lightweight linen clothes, while wool was more suitable in winter.

All but the most wealthy made their own clothes, consisting of a simple tunic (called a **CHITON**) and a draped cloak, or **HIMATION** (picture ④). Both men and women wore basically the same style. The women spun and then wove the cloth. They then bleached the material to make it white, and finally dyed it using natural dyes (usually indigo, madder or saffron) to match the colours of their home state.

The Greeks also wore hats, using them while travelling to keep the sunshine away. They were held on with a chinstrap and could hang down the back when not needed.

It was quite common to walk about barefoot. For travelling, people wore thin sandals.

People kept clean by a mixture of scraping their bodies with a dull metal blade and by applying perfumes they made by boiling up flowers and scented leaves.

A peplos was a tubular garment, often worn over a chiton and fastened by pins at the shoulders.

A himation was a kind of cloak. It was a rectangle of wool with weighted corners, slung over the left shoulder, leaving the right arm free. It was worn by men and women. It also served as a blanket. The colours were mostly white, natural, browns, and black.

(Greeks believed that a pale complexion was a sign of beauty and so they tried not to become too suntanned.)

## Married life

A girl would be married off by her parents in an arranged marriage at about 15 years of age. She would be taken to her husband's house in a chariot which would then be broken up as a sign that she could never go home again. After this the wife would rarely go out of the home and she always did what her husband said. But she did have complete control over the household and the slaves.

◀ ⑤ The ancient Greeks wore many fashionable hairstyles. This sculpture shows a man with short, wavy hair combed down over the forehead. Wealthy women wore long hair set in braids. They also had pony tails and held their hair in place with ribbons wound around the head. Otherwise the hair was set in place using scented waxes. Ancient Greeks did not have fair hair, but thought that it was an attractive feature, so they tried bleaching their hair.

▼ ④ Clothing styles.

A chiton was made of a square of cloth, held in place by brooches and pins at the shoulders and a belt round the waist.

A chlamys was a square of wool worn by men and pinned over the right shoulder. It might be worn with a short chiton and by young men with no other clothing.

Weblink: www.CurriculumVisions.com

# Theatre, myths and fables

The theatre was invented in ancient Greece. It was a mixture of religious festival, acting, dancing, singing and music.

For most of the time people entertained themselves at home by telling stories around the fire. But in Athens, in about 500 BC, the Greeks also invented the theatre. The word drama comes from Greek words meaning 'to do' or 'to act'. A play is a story acted out, often exaggerating some part of human life.

Plays began as a way of honouring the gods (picture ②). The first plays were written for a festival in honour of the god Dionysus, the god of fertility and wine. Attending the festival and listening to the plays was regarded as an act of worship.

## The theatre building

A Greek theatre building, or *theatron*, (amphitheatre) was open to the sky (Greek summers being rainless). It consisted of three parts: the orchestra, the skene and the audience (picture ③).

At the centre was the orchestra, which at this time meant the place where the play was read out as well as where the religious ceremonies took place. It was a large circular area about 150 metres across with a floor of beaten earth. At its centre was an altar.

Behind the orchestra circle was a large rectangular building called the skene, meaning tent, because originally it was just a tent put up during the festival. It was used as the actors' changing room. Later, the skenes became permanent buildings and often had backdrops painted on them, giving us the word scenery.

The audience sat on rows of stone benches built up on the side of a hollow in a hill. So theatres could not just be built anywhere, they had to be built where the landscape was suitable. A typical theatre could seat 15,000.

Greek plays involved song, chant, and dance together with musical accompaniment (picture ①).

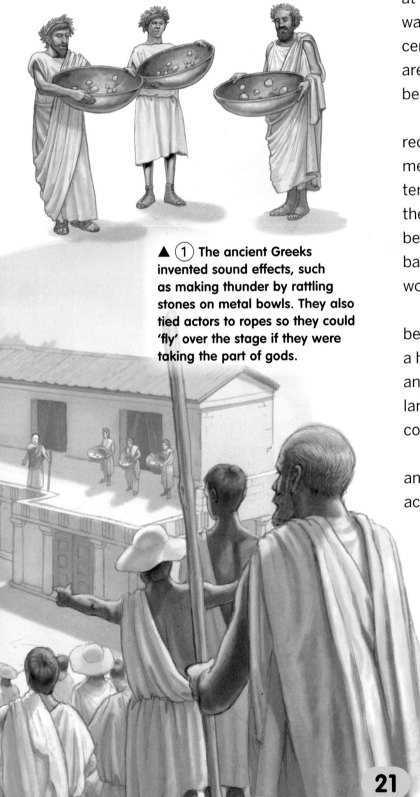

▲ ① **The ancient Greeks invented sound effects, such as making thunder by rattling stones on metal bowls. They also tied actors to ropes so they could 'fly' over the stage if they were taking the part of gods.**

◄ ② **Plays took a long time to act out. People would bring their own food. If they enjoyed the performance they would whistle and stamp their feet. If they did not enjoy the play they would boo and even throw food and stones. The theatre employed stewards with long sticks who would beat up the audience if it became too rowdy!**

## Plays

Some plays were designed to make people laugh (comedies) and others told stories with sad endings (tragedies).

Tragedies were more popular. Most Greek tragedies are based on mythology or history and deal with characters' search for the meaning of life and the nature of the gods. Historical plays were often based on stories involving wars between the Greek cities and their Persian neighbours. In these stories the hero saves the city, but dies in doing so.

## Actors

All of the actors were either men or boys. They would also play the parts of women. The story would also have a narrator or a chorus, who carried the story on when the actors were not speaking.

In 534 BC, a man called Thespis was the first to speak and act as though he were the character, rather than just recite the words. This is why Thespis is thought of as the first Greek 'actor' and why actors today are sometimes called thespians.

## Masks

The same actor might also play several parts, showing which part he was playing by changing masks. The masks were made of linen or cork. A double mask is still the symbol for the theatre.

## Playwrights

Many people must have written plays, but much of their work has been lost. The most famous ancient Greek playwrights are Sophocles and Euripides.

## Sponsors

Putting on a play, making the costumes and masks and so on was an expensive business and so the wealthiest citizens sponsored the events by providing money. Sponsorship is still common today.

## Myths and fables

Myths and fables are stories handed down by word of mouth over many centuries. Myths are stories about the fantastic exploits of gods and heroes. Fables, on the other hand, are gentler stories, usually involving animals, and designed to point out a truth – or moral – at the end. The most famous are called *Aesop's fables*, possibly

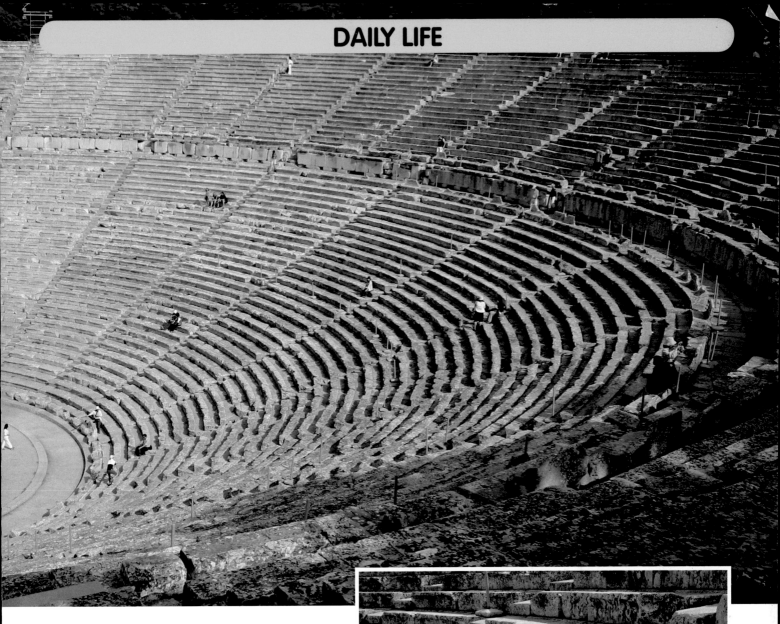

written by Aesop, a slave and storyteller living in ancient Greece in the 6th century BC.

Today we think of a hero as somebody who does something dangerous to help somebody else. But Greek heroes were not at all like this – although they had great courage and strength, and were favoured by the gods, they were a pretty selfish bunch.

The story of *Jason and the Argonauts* is a classic myth that was written by Apollonius of Rhodes in the third century BC. He was not the first to tell the story, but his version is the best known today (see page 24).

▲ ③ This is the famous theatre at Epidauros. It was part of a temple sanctuary. It could hold 14,000 people. The seats in the lower part are more roomy while the upper section has smaller seats (the cheap seats). As a result, the top half is slightly steeper than the bottom.

Weblink: www.CurriculumVisions.com

# The myth of Jason, the Argonauts and the Golden Fleece

Jason is the son of a king. But the country has been taken over by his power-hungry brother Pelias. Fearing that her son would be killed by Pelias, Jason's mother sends him away to live in the cave of Chiron the Centaur (half man, half horse), where he is raised until he is a man. Then Jason returns to claim the throne. But on his way back, he is tested by the goddess Hera. Disguised as an elderly woman, Hera begs Jason to help her across a stream. He agrees and takes her on his back. Jason's goodwill impresses Hera, and she makes it her duty to help him on his journey.

## The Argo

Jason meets with Pelias and says the throne is rightfully his. Pelias agrees to give up the throne providing Jason can bring back the Golden Fleece. Pelius doesn't think this is possible. But Jason builds a boat called the Argo and gets a crew of heroes, such as Herakles. Jason calls this crew the Argonauts.

The Argonauts set sail for the land of the Golden Fleece. The ship first stops at an island where there are only women. Herakles wants to go no further and is left behind.

## The Clashing Rocks

The Argo makes its way to another island, where the crew chases flying witches away. To show his gratitude, King Phineus warns them that they will soon meet the Clashing Rocks. The rocks clash together whenever a ship tries to get through. The secret, Phineus says, is to release a bird between the rocks so that they come together, then, before they have time to clash again, the Argo can sail through. As a result, the Argo gets safely to the land of the Golden Fleece.

## The Golden Fleece

Aeetes, the king where the Fleece is kept, dislikes Jason but agrees to give him the Golden Fleece if he could help out with a few small jobs. These jobs are seemingly impossible tasks designed to kill Jason. Fortunately for Jason, the goddess Aphrodite makes Medea, the king's daughter, fall in love with Jason. Medea has magical powers which she uses to help Jason complete the jobs. First Jason is ordered to harness two fire-breathing bulls. He then has to plant some dragon's teeth in a field. As the teeth enter the soil, they sprout into armed warriors. Without Medea's assistance, Jason would have been killed, but thanks to her magic he harnesses the bulls and kills the warriors.

Jason now finds that the Fleece is guarded by a dragon. The dragon is given a sleeping potion by Medea and Jason grabs the Fleece. The Argonauts quickly set sail but they are pursued by the king's army. On the return trip to Greece, the Argo is safely guided with help from Hera. Medea then kills Pelias and Jason becomes king. As you can see, it all ends happily ever after!

## Herakles
## – a Greek hero

Herakles (whose name means 'to the glory of (goddess) Hera') is one of the most famous ancient Greek heroes. He is a muscle-man who is famous for his super-human strength. (The Romans changed his name to Hercules when they took over Greek myths).

To become a hero Herakles had to perform these tasks:

❶ Conquer and deliver a monster.

❷ Kill the multi-headed Hydra.

❸ Bring back, dead or alive, a fierce deer.

❹ Catch a huge boar.

❺ Clean out the massive stables of Augeas.

❻ Scare off and kill the metal-feathered Stymphalian birds.

❼ Capture the Cretan Bull.

❽ Do something about the man-eating Mares of Diomedes (he moved them and released them).

❾ Get the Girdle of Hippolyta, Queen of the Amazons (she gave it to him peacefully, which enraged Hera, who arranged for the rest of the Amazons to attack Herakles; in the mess that followed, Hippolyta was killed by Herakles.)

❿ Steal the cattle of Geryon.

⓫ Bring back the Golden Apples of the Hesperides.

⓬ Go down to the underworld and bring back multi-headed Cerberus, chief hound of the underworld god, Hades.

He did all this before embarking on the Argo with Jason.

▲ Herakles captures the Cretan Bull.

◀▶ Atlas (right) offering Herakles the Golden Apples of the Hesperides. Herakles holds the sky on his shoulder, assisted by Athena (left).

# Schooling in ancient Greece

**All cities believed that is was important to train children. This was also a time of war, so learning and war training were mixed together.**

We live in relatively safe times and only small numbers of the military are needed to defend us. But in ancient Greek times this was not so. All citizens had to know how to defend their city, and so military training was part of every school – although it was often in the form of fitness and games.

Here are two examples to show you how different ancient Greek schooling could be between cities and in comparison with our schools today.

## Schooling in Athens

Athens was a city that was proud of its education, its arts and its music. But they also realised that they had to defend themselves. So their schooling was in three stages with military training at the end (picture ①). Very young children were taught at home, often by a slave.

When they were about six, boys went to school, while girls continued to be taught at home.

▶ Greek has 24 letters, as opposed to the 26 in modern English. These letters are used today throughout the world as mathematical symbols.

| | | |
|---|---|---|
| Αα | alpha | a |
| Ββ | beta | b |
| Γγ | gamma | g |
| Δδ | delta | d |
| Εε | epsilon | e |
| Ζζ | zeta | z |
| Ηη | eta | e |
| Θθ | theta | th |
| Ιι | iota | i |
| Κκ | kappa | k |
| Λλ | lambda | l |
| Μμ | mu | m |
| Νν | nu | n |
| Ξξ | xi | x (ks) |
| Οο | omicron | o |
| Ππ | pi | p |
| Ρρ | rho | r |
| Σσ | sigma | s |
| Ττ | tau | t |
| Υυ | upsilon | u, y |
| Φφ | phi | ph |
| Χχ | chi | kh, ch |
| Ψψ | psi | ps |
| Ωω | omega | o |

Books were rare, expensive things that had to be produced by hand. So the boys had to memorise everything they learned. They also spent much of their time doing healthy exercise.

Athenian boys learned the works of the poet Homer, and they also learned to play a musical instrument, often the lyre.

▶ ① Athenian boys had wax tablets and pointed sticks which they used to learn to write (schools in Britain used the same kind of system (slate and chalk) into the 20th century).

The teacher also taught public speaking, ideas of government and anything else he wanted.

◄ ② Spartan children were taught fighting and survival skills (see page 32). Only after this were there extra classes in reading and writing.

When they reached 18 years of age, all boys had to go into military school until the age of 20.

## Schooling in Sparta

Sparta was proud of its simple, tough life, with none of what they saw as the sloppiness of Athens. The Spartans put self-defence before other kinds of education.

Spartans didn't believe they could support weak citizens of a city, so if a baby was weak it was allowed to die on the mountains, or perhaps trained to be a slave.

Early schooling was done at home, as in Athens, but at about 6 years of age both boys and girls started school, living in army barracks (picture ②).

At about 18, when the Athenians were about to start army training, the Spartans would have been in the army for 12 to 13 years and were ready to face their passing-out test. Only those who passed this test became full citizens and Spartan soldiers. Spartan girls who passed the test could return home and become married to a Spartan soldier.

### The gymnasium: Greek university

The gymnasium was a special kind of school complex, effectively a kind of sporting university. In Athens, for example, there were three great public gymnasia, named Academy, Lyceum and Cynosarges. The gymnasium trained men from the age of 18 in bodily health, the best of whom would represent the city in the Olympic Games (see page 44). It was named gymnasium because the competitors exercised, wrestled and boxed without clothes on (gymnos means naked). It was also a place where they bathed together (a bit like Roman baths).

The gymnasium developed because the Greeks thought highly of perfect physical bodies, exercise and health. But it was also a place where the students could listen to the great thinkers of the day.

The gymnasium did not survive Greek times. Although the Romans took on many things that the Greeks valued, they did not continue with the gymnasium because they did not think it was useful as army training. However, the word gymnasium remains in many European countries as a place of teaching excellence. In the UK it is used simply to mean a place of exercise.

# Art and design

The ancient Greeks developed ways of painting, sculpting and designing buildings that we have copied to the present time.

For about 900 years the ancient Greeks developed a style of art that was unique. It was copied by the Romans, and is still copied today.

## Pottery

Nearly all Greek pottery was made for use in the home. It was decorated with people and scenes using black, white, red and yellow glazes (picture ①). Surviving pieces of pottery tell us much about the way the ancient Greeks lived.

◀ ① **Greek pottery showing runners at the Olympic Games.**

## Sculpture

Greek sculpture was meant for public memorials, and as offerings (picture ②) in religious buildings such as temples.

The ancient Greeks were very interested in the human body (picture ③). They tried to show off what they thought were the best features of the body to make sculptures which were pleasing to their eyes.

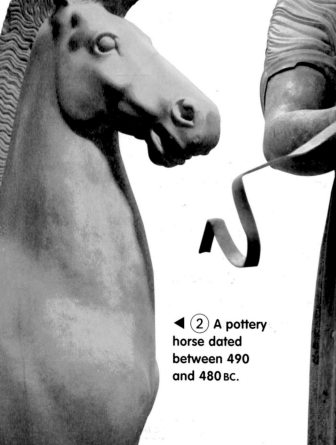

◀ ② **A pottery horse dated between 490 and 480 BC.**

◀ ③ **The Charioteer of Delphi, Delphi Archaeological Museum. One of the greatest surviving works of Greek sculpture, it dates from about 470 BC. This bronze is in the Early Classical style, and it is one of the few Greek statues to have kept its inlaid glass eyes.**

Ionic column design

④ There were two main styles of Greek architecture, called DORIC and IONIC.

The Doric style was very simple, and a little squat and sturdy, whereas the Ionic style was thinner, more elegant and decorative.

Most of the best known surviving Greek buildings are Doric.

Doric          Ionic

Detail at base of Ionic column.

The largest object the Greeks ever sculpted was the Colossus of Rhodes (late 3rd century), which was the same size as New York's Statue of Liberty. It was one of the Seven Wonders of the Ancient World.

## Buildings

The Greeks were wealthy enough to pay for large buildings as early as the 7th century BC. However, these were made in wood and mud brick and have not survived. So we only really know of what the Greeks made in later periods, when they began to use stone.

There was a basic design to all of the buildings. They were either a square or a rectangle. If they were rectangular, then the sides were proportioned according to a shape called the golden rectangle (page 15). They were almost always made from limestone or marble.

At the front they added a porch with a roof supported by many columns, providing a grand entrance.

Because the Greeks, like the ancient Egyptians, did not use arches or domes, they could not build large rooms with unsupported roofs: any large building needed rows of internal columns to hold the roof up (picture ④). All of their buildings have simple flat or gently sloping roofs. The end of each roof (the pediment) was filled in and then decorated with sculptures. The space just below the roof line (the frieze) was also decorated with sculptures (see page 13).

# City states: Athens and Sparta

**Athens and Sparta were the largest cities in ancient Greece, and they were rivals.**

Sparta and Athens were the biggest and most powerful of the Greek cities – and they had completely different ideas of how to live.

Athens, just a few kilometres from the sea, is now the capital of modern Greece. In ancient Greek times it was the richest city in Greece, based on trade using its fleet of ships. Sparta was a city in the southernmost part of the Greek mainland. Unlike Athens, Sparta was not near the sea. So it developed an army, rather than a navy.

### Rich Athens

Athens was the largest of the city states in ancient Greece. It may have had a population as large as 300,000. (At this time the biggest city in Britain had just a few hundred people!)

Athens also controlled the fertile land around it, forming a region called Attica. Within the land of Attica there were also gold, silver and lead mines and marble quarries. This made Athens a very rich city. Because it was also close to the sea, it could trade these precious metals and rocks for the extra food it needed beyond what its own land could provide. The port for Athens was called Pireus.

Athens became so wealthy from trade and the spoils of wars that it could spend large sums of money on the best artists and builders of the time.

City walls

Athens

Pireus

Athens began on a natural hill of white limestone rock about 7 km from the sea. It was a good site and easy to defend. Today it is called the Acropolis, meaning highest city. But Athens outgrew its Acropolis and so new houses were built on the plain below. Over time, the hill was turned into a religious sanctuary. It was flattened off and great temples were built on it, including the most famous building of Greek times, the Parthenon.

## Democracy

Athens was first run by kings, then by nobles, then by a single general called a TYRANT.

In 510 BC the people tried a new experiment in running their city by giving its male citizens (but not women) the right to vote for their leaders (picture ①).

Athens also developed new ways of dealing with criminals using public law courts and trials by juries comprising hundreds of people. The jurors voted by placing discs in one of two jars – one for guilty, one for not guilty.

## Slaves

Like other Greek cities, Athens was run on slave labour. A third of all people living in Athens were slaves. Some slaves were children of slaves, while the stock of slaves was added to by capturing people during wars.

Slaves were not necessarily the poorest and least educated of people. Although slaves did work in the mines and at rock breaking, and toiled in the fields, teachers and nurses, for example, might also be slaves. Even those who kept the peace (the Athenian form of a police force) were slave archers from Scythia.

▼ ① Any free man (citizen) could go to the assembly, where they could speak and vote freely. When there was disagreement, people held public debates.

## Festivals and leisure

The citizens of Athens had the time, the money and the imagination to do things other than work. There were yearly festivals to honour gods, athletics competitions and a season of plays.

Rich citizens were happy to be asked to pay for the performers, just as companies and rich people might sponsor events today.

## Fighting Spartans

In the early part of the 6th century Sparta was defeated by neighbouring cities and the people decided that this was because, as people, they were too weak and not fit enough to defend themselves. So, from that time, the idea of extreme fitness and a city of soldiers developed.

Sparta chose not to have walls to defend itself. Without walls people knew they had to be tough and well trained all of the time – including women and children.

You can see how this made Sparta a very different place from Athens. No grand buildings, art and writing here. Instead it looked like a group of villages with a lean and mean military rule that everyone else feared. This was also important because Sparta controlled a bigger state than any other city – and much of it had been captured from its neighbours, so there was always the risk of rebellion.

The city of Sparta was like one vast army. It put fitness and strength ahead of reading and the arts, so the people left no written records of themselves.

In the writings that have come down to us, there is hardly a good word to be said for the Spartans, but this is less surprising when we realise that all of this writing was done by their arch-rivals, the Athenians. The Spartans believed their way was the best, and many of their Greek neighbours agreed with them.

## Growing up in Sparta

The ordinary Spartan was essentially a soldier, trained to obey and endure. Shortly after birth, children were brought before the elders of the state, who decided whether it was to be reared or not. If found sick or weak, the baby was dropped off a cliff called the Place of Rejection, or left to die in the mountains. In this way the Spartans followed the rule of the Survival of the Fittest.

Boys were taken from their families at the age of six and trained in the art of warfare in the mountains. They were only allowed a cloak, no other clothes and no shoes. They were also given too little food, so they had to try to steal food from the farms – and if they were caught they were beaten. The point of this was that, in battle conditions, food is often not easy to come by, and so you have to know how to get by on little or to find it from somewhere. Spartan boys were not allowed back to their families until they were 20 – so they spent thirteen years being hardened up.

Girls in Sparta did not escape training. They too were taken from their families and trained. The idea was to produce strong women who could have healthy babies and who also knew how to fight if needed.

Girls were found a husband when they were 18 and then they could return home. But there was another side to this. Whereas in other cities women were kept in their homes all of the time, Spartan women could move around freely – in part because their husbands would not live at home until they were in their thirties, but lived in army barracks instead.

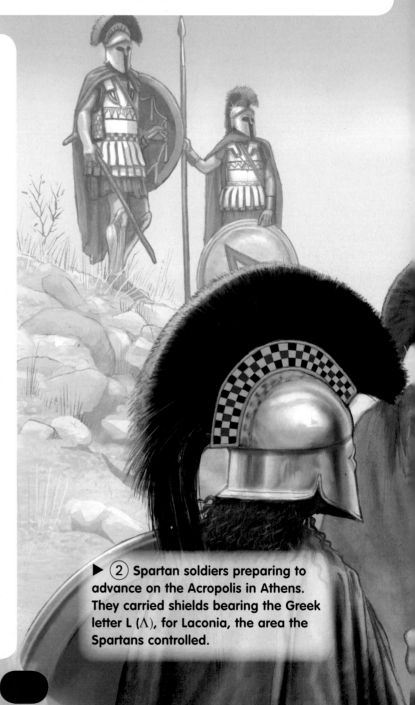

▶ ② Spartan soldiers preparing to advance on the Acropolis in Athens. They carried shields bearing the Greek letter L (Λ), for Laconia, the area the Spartans controlled.

## Sparta versus Athens

When not being attacked by their powerful neighbours, the Persians, Athens and Sparta turned on each other. But it was not easy for one state to win out over the other. This is because Athens had a stronger navy and Sparta a stronger army. When Sparta attacked, Athens retreated behind its walls and supplied itself with food using its ships.

Eventually, the Athenians and the Spartans got involved in a thirty year war (called the Peloponnesian War). They slogged it out between themselves for so long that, in the end they were like two punch drunk fighters. Both were fatally weakened, although in the end the Spartans won and forced the Athenians to pull down their city walls.

But these self-inflicted wounds meant that neither Athens nor Sparta could be powerful again, and it was left to a king from the north to rule both cities and far more. This would be Alexander the Great.

# The ancient Greeks at war

**The ancient Greek land was made of many city states that fought with each other and with neighbouring countries. As a result, the Greeks trained hard and developed new skills in fighting.**

▶ ① **Shield with** *episema* **symbol.**

Greek cities often faced threats of invasion from overseas or attack by neighbouring states. As a result learning to fight was taken very seriously (picture ②). When they became soldiers, men gave a sacred military oath in front of their shields (picture ①). In Sparta, soldiers gave oaths to die before surrendering.

It was shameful to lose a battle and come back with your shield, and even worse to have lost your shield to the enemy. However, it was thought glorious to be carried back dead on your shield. Spartan mothers would say to their sons as they left for battle: "Come back with your shield – or on it!" Because Spartan soldiers had given this oath, they were especially ferocious warriors and immensely feared.

▼ ② **The Greeks fought mainly with long spears and swords. During an attack they locked shields to form a solid protective wall, with each soldier placing his shield over the soldier to his left. They lined up eight or more deep – called a PHALANX.**

## What armies looked like

The Greeks were all of the same race, so they all looked alike. So how did the soldiers know who was on their side and who was the enemy? How did they know where their commander was?

The ancient Greek armies did not use flags or uniforms, but put symbols (which they called *episema*) on their shields (picture ①). They used symbols such as an owl (Athens) or an eagle (Macedonians) or pictures of gods. The Spartans used the Greek letter L (Λ) on their shields, which stands for Laconia, the name of the area surrounding Sparta.

## Hoplites – the Greek shock troops

The heavily-armoured soldier in any Greek army was known as a **HOPLITE** (picture ④). Hoplites were citizens, and as such were responsible for defending their city. Each hoplite had to pay for his own equipment, so they used nothing fancy or expensive (picture ③). The total cost of the gear was roughly equivalent to a middle-sized car in our time.

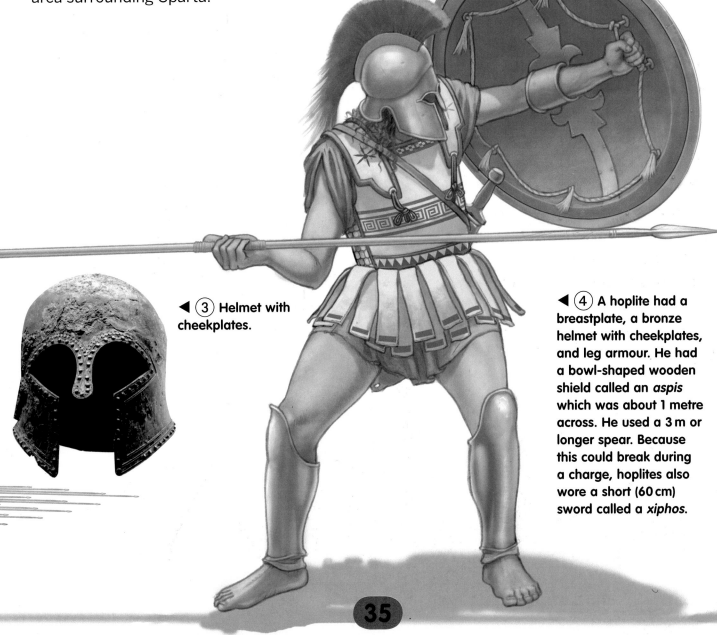

◀ ③ Helmet with cheekplates.

◀ ④ A hoplite had a breastplate, a bronze helmet with cheekplates, and leg armour. He had a bowl-shaped wooden shield called an *aspis* which was about 1 metre across. He used a 3 m or longer spear. Because this could break during a charge, hoplites also wore a short (60 cm) sword called a *xiphos*.

▲▶ ⑤ (left) The site of the Battle of Marathon. (right) How the Athenians beat the Persians.

▶ ⑥ Hand to hand fighting as the Athenians force the Persians back to their ships at the end of the Battle of Marathon.

## Tactics

The Persians tended to wear relatively light armour, had shorter spears and smaller shields.

At the start of a battle the two armies would run into each other in the hope of breaking the enemy line. Then it was a pushing match, with the men at the back trying to force their front lines through those of the enemy.

Battles rarely lasted more than an hour or so. Once one of the lines broke, the troops would generally drop their equipment and flee from the field.

## Famous Greek battles

The ancient Greeks fought two battles that are among the most important ever fought in western history. The first was a land battle called the Battle of Marathon (pictures ⑤ and ⑥). The second was fought at sea and was the Battle of Salamis. Both battles were fought against the Persians.

## The Battle of Marathon

The Greeks were always weakened by the fact that the city states hated one another. King Darius of Persia thought he could take advantage of this. If he was right, he could first destroy Athens and then advance on to Sparta.

In 490 BC he began his campaign. His army landed at the Bay of Marathon, about 40 km north east of Athens. What he wanted to do was to persuade the Athenian army, who had retreated behind their defensive walls, to flee the city.

The Athenians did not think they could defeat Darius and so they sent an urgent message for help. They sent

KEY
Persians
Athenians

1

2

3

Final note: Pheidippides did not run to Athens (about 40 km away), as some popular stories tell. The modern marathon is based on a story invented by Plutarch in the 1st century AD and the distance was only decided on about 100 years ago (see page 43). It has nothing to do with the distance Pheidippides actually ran.

the courier Pheidippides to the Spartans. That was 300 km away!

When Pheidippides arrived in Sparta the Spartans explained that they could not go to war until their religious festival had ended about ten days later. How could the Athenians hold out so long?

When the Athenian army learned that the Persians had landed at Marathon, they went to meet them. The Athenians simply stood their ground while they waited for the Spartans. As a result, for eight days the armies peacefully confronted each other.

But then the Athenians decided to attack because most of the Persian army were archers who fought

at a distance whereas the Greeks had javelins and so they needed to get up close.

The Greeks tried to surround the Persians even though they had fewer troops. So the wings went ahead faster than the middle. The Greek centre then gave way, and the Persians rushed forwards, allowing the Greeks to encircle them. Now the Greeks' spears and heavy armour made it possible for them to beat the Persians. The Persians panicked and fled.

It was the first time the Greeks had won against the Persians. This made the Greeks confident in themselves and so allowed Greek (western) civilisation to continue.

# The Battle of Salamis

All of the countries of the Mediterranean had GALLEYS, ships which relied for their speed on banks of oarsmen. The sails were not used in battle. The biggest of these – perhaps 75 m long – had three banks of oars and were called TRIREMES (tri means three). They carried about 200 people, the great majority of whom were oarsmen. Each boat carried a small number of soldiers for hand to hand fighting when ships came close together.

The Greeks, and especially the Athenians (who were the main seagoing city in Greece) were proud of their ships. But the Persians had by far the biggest fleet in the Mediterranean.

They also had the biggest and fastest boats.

The Battle of Salamis is a 'David and Goliath' story. Here the Greeks are tiny David, and the Persians under King Xerxes are gigantic Goliath. The Greeks were outnumbered in ships by three to one and so if they were to win, it had to be through cunning – and the overconfidence of the Persians.

This is what happened. The Persians had sailed over the Aegean Sea and burned the city of Athens. In fear of their lives, the Athenians had fled to the island of Salamis. The Greek fleet tried to beat the Persians, but it was a standoff and so they, too, retreated to Salamis.

Meanwhile, the Spartans wanted to go back to Sparta, where they thought they stood a better chance of keeping the Persians at bay. But the Athenian commander, Themistocles, persuaded them to remain at Salamis. He was able to do this because of the prophecy by the oracle at Delphi which said that Salamis would "bring death to women's sons," but also that the Greeks would be saved by

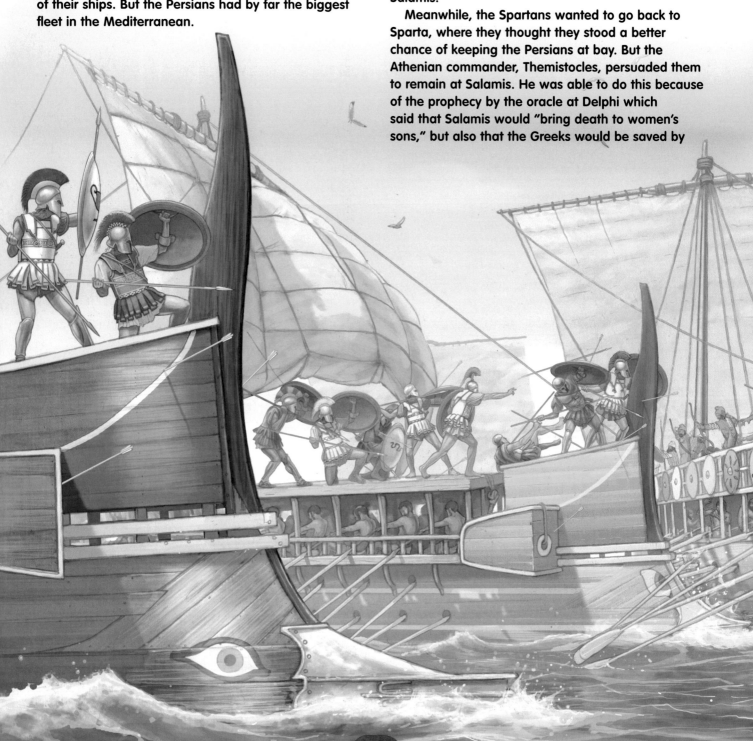

a "wooden wall". Themistocles said that the wooden wall was a fleet of ships, and Salamis would bring death to the Persians, not the Greeks.

King Xerxes expected an easy victory. Xerxes knew that the Greek navy was hiding at Salamis. Themistocles sent out a slave who pretended he had run away from the Greeks. He told Xerxes that the Greeks could not decide what to do and the navy was about to flee. Xerxes wanted to crush the Greek navy once and for all, and so he sent his navy looking for them. They looked all night and were exhausted. But they found no ships because Thermistocles had his ships still in harbour waiting.

The next morning the Persians sailed in to the straits to attack the Greek fleet. Part of the Greek fleet then pretended to retreat, luring the Persians farther into the narrow straits (picture ⑦).

Then the Greeks attacked. The much larger Persian fleet could not turn in the straits. The Persians tried to turn back, but there were now too many of them jammed into the straits. The Greek and Persian ships rammed each other (picture ⑥).

At least 200 Persian ships were sunk. But the Persians could not swim, so as each boat sank, the men drowned.

Because the Battle of Salamis saved Greece from becoming part of the Persian empire, it meant that the Persians never conquered Europe. Many historians have therefore called the Battle of Salamis one of the most important battles of all time.

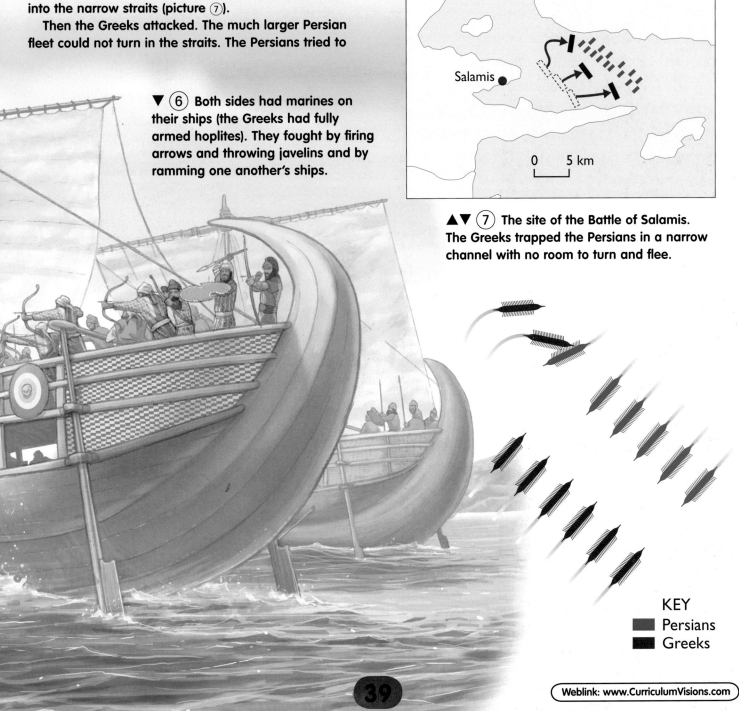

▼ ⑥ Both sides had marines on their ships (the Greeks had fully armed hoplites). They fought by firing arrows and throwing javelins and by ramming one another's ships.

▲▼ ⑦ The site of the Battle of Salamis. The Greeks trapped the Persians in a narrow channel with no room to turn and flee.

Salamis

0    5 km

KEY
■ Persians
■ Greeks

39

# The Olympic Games

**The Olympic Games lasted for nearly 1,200 years. They were a place where ancient rival city states could do battle peacefully.**

The word athlete comes from the ancient Greek meaning 'someone who competes for a prize'.

Contests between the fittest men had taken place for centuries before the Olympic Games started. But these were local affairs. The Olympic Games became special because it attracted people from all over the ancient Greek empire.

The Olympic Games may have come about through the ancient Greek idea of truce. You have to remember that, at this time, wars between cities in Greece were common. For a month before the Olympic Games started, all of the Greek cities would stop warring with one another and take part in games held on neutral territory in the countryside, at the sanctuary for Zeus at Olympia (known as the Altis). By attracting Greeks from all over the ancient Greek world, the games also helped to hold the Greek empire together.

## The games develop

The first recorded games at Olympia date from about 776 BC, although they were held for a long time before this, perhaps as early as the 10th or 9th century BC. But we do know that from 776 BC games were held in Olympia every four years for almost 1,200 years.

At first the Olympic Games lasted just one day and there was just one event – the 200 m sprint from one end of the race track to the other – and known as the **STADION** (picture ③, page 43). The stadion race track can still be seen in Olympia.

But as the years went by the games lengthened to last five days and include eight competitions: chariot racing, boxing, wrestling, running, armed combat, discus, archery and javelin. The Olympic Games were held every four years, and the period between the games was called an **OLYMPIAD**. The Greeks used Olympiads as one of their methods to count years.

▼ ① **What remains of the sculptures from the pediment on the temple of Zeus.**

### Old and modern ideas

In ancient Greece, the Olympic Games were about fame and glory – but also about wealth and money. The ancient Greeks trained so hard they were really professionals. So the modern games, with its ideas of 'amateurs' competing just for honour and not for money, would have seemed very strange to the ancient Greeks. The idea of the amateur developed only in the 19th century AD.

The most famous Olympic athlete, the sixth century BC wrestler Milo of Croton is the only athlete in history to win a victory in six Olympics.

## Fierce competition

The Olympics were of religious importance, and sporting contests alternated with sacrifices and ceremonies honouring both Zeus (whose colossal statue stood at Olympia) (pictures ① and ②), and Pelops, divine hero and famous for a legendary chariot race, in whose honour the games were held.

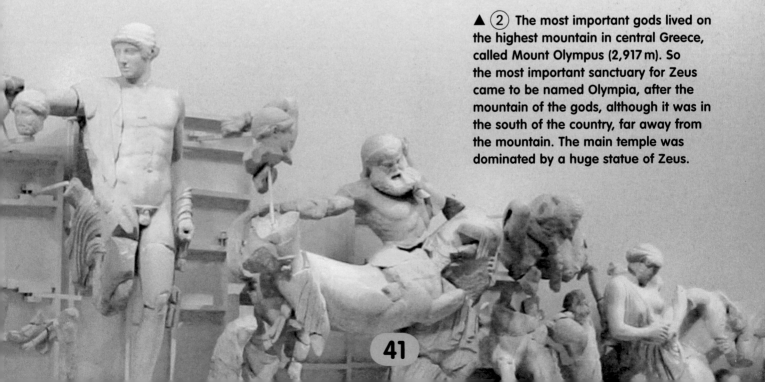

▲ ② The most important gods lived on the highest mountain in central Greece, called Mount Olympus (2,917 m). So the most important sanctuary for Zeus came to be named Olympia, after the mountain of the gods, although it was in the south of the country, far away from the mountain. The main temple was dominated by a huge statue of Zeus.

Only young men competed. The competitors were naked, in part because the weather was hot in Greece, but also because the games celebrated the achievements of the human body.

The games were not friendly competitions as we know them today, but a bitter rivalry among the city states of the Greek world. Whoever won each contest was given a simple crown of olive leaves that came from a wild olive tree in the Altis. But the main prize was fame and honour to the winner's city. Poems were written about the winners of the games, they had statues made of them, and they were cheered in the streets. They also usually became very rich.

## Women's games

Only men, boys and unmarried girls were allowed to attend the Olympic Games. Women caught sneaking in faced a severe punishment!

Women did have their own festival at Olympia once every four years. It was called the Heraia and was held in honour of Hera, wife of Zeus.

The main temple was in honour of Zeus.

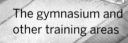

The gymnasium and other training areas

# THE OLYMPIC GAMES

## The stadion

During the Olympic Games people would sleep in tents around the stadion. The stadion was 200 metres long and 30 metres wide. It was in a valley, with rows of seats sloping up the hillside on either side, and the starting line for the athletes was marked by a line of stones set into the ground. The surface of the stadion was white sand.

## The modern marathon

The modern marathon is one of the most famous Olympic events. The race commemorates the amazing journey of the runner Pheidippides who carried the news that the Persian army had landed at the coastal city of Marathon, north east of Athens, to Sparta 300 km away (see page 37).

However, the marathon was not part of the ancient Greek Olympics. It is a modern event that was introduced in the first modern Olympic Games in Athens in 1896. On that date the marathon was a race from Marathon to the Olympic stadium, just 40 kilometres. The standardised marathon is 26 miles 385 yards or 42.2 km. It was established in 1908 when the Olympic Games were held in London. This was the distance between Windsor Castle, the start of the race, and the finish line inside London's White City Stadium.

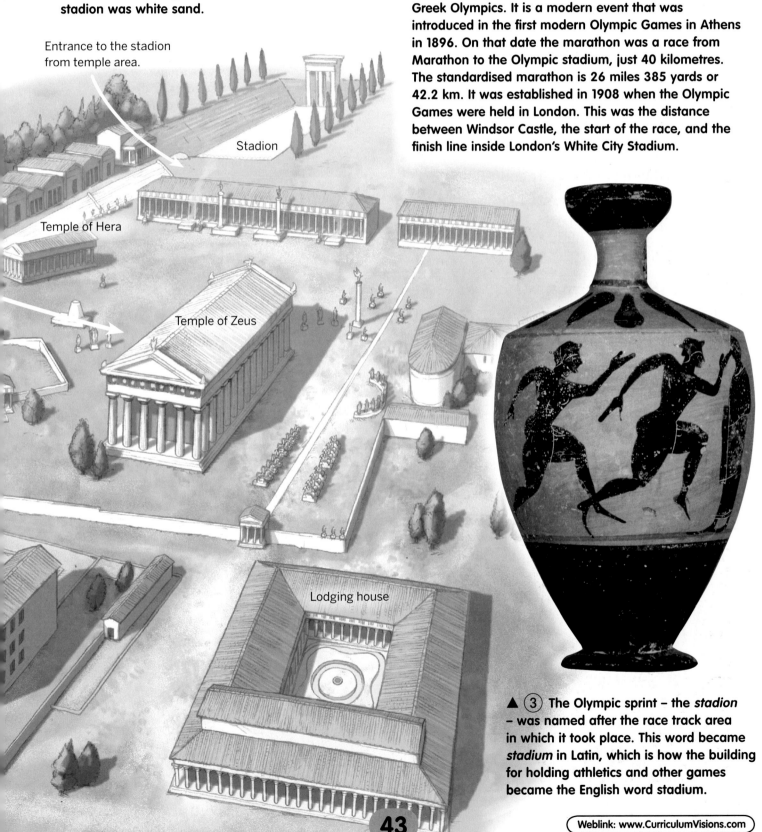

Entrance to the stadion from temple area.

Stadion

Temple of Hera

Temple of Zeus

Lodging house

▲ ③ The Olympic sprint – the *stadion* – was named after the race track area in which it took place. This word became *stadium* in Latin, which is how the building for holding athletics and other games became the English word stadium.

43

The events were all running races, and unmarried girls took part. Winners were awarded crowns of sacred olive branches, the same as men.

## What happened to the ancient Olympics?

The ancient games were staged in Olympia, Greece, from 776 BC until 393 AD. When Christianity became the official religion of the Roman empire, the Olympic Games were seen as a pagan festival threatening Christianity, which is why the emperor Theodosius outlawed them, ending nearly 1,200 years of tradition. The games were then abandoned for 1,503 years.

## The modern games

Many of the features of the ancient games have been used for the modern games, although there are, of course, strict safety rules, no sacrifices and many more events taking place over a longer period.

The first modern Olympics were held in Athens, Greece, in 1896. The man responsible for restarting the games was the Frenchman Baron Pierre de Coubertin. His original idea was to have the modern games in Paris in 1900 to mark the start of the new century, but international pressure forced him to start the games in 1896 in Athens. Paris did become the second host, in 1900, and the games have been held every four years since then (except for wartime breaks).

### Olympic torch

There was no relay of torch bearers in the ancient Olympic Games, although there had been other torch relays in ancient Greek times. The idea of a relay from the city of Olympia in Greece to the host city to start the games came into being at the 1936 Olympic Games in Berlin.

▼ ④ A boxing match from the ancient Greek Olympic Games as shown on the side of a large vase (amphora). In ancient Greek times all of the games were played without clothes.

## Events of an Olympiad

### Training

The athletes had to be trained in their home city for ten months before the games. They arrived at least one month before the festival took place. At the same time, messengers wearing crowns of olive leaves went to the Greek cities to proclaim the truce, which lasted for three months.

### Day One

The ceremony started with the athletes' registration and the official oath of the competitors and judges. In front of the statue of Zeus, the athletes had to swear that they had been trained for the last ten months and would obey the rules during the games. The judges then had to swear to judge fairly. The games were opened by a procession of athletes and judges.

The first competition was between the trumpeters and the heralds. The winners had the honour to announce the names of the victors and sound the trumpet for all events at Olympia.

This was, of course, a religious ceremony and so sacrifices were made to the gods at their altars.

### Day Two

This was the day of the first competition.

First was the *stadion* race – the sprint from one end of the stadium to the other, about 200 m.

The next competition was wrestling (picture ⑦), then boxing (picture ④) and then the pankration (pronounced pan/cray/shun) matches. These were a brutal, all-out combat (which today we would call martial arts) which were as close to no-holds-barred fighting that any people has ever allowed. Only biting and gouging were prohibited. Kicking was an essential part of pankration.

### Day Three

On this day the events involving horses and the pentathlon (five event) occurred. They included two (picture ⑥) and four-horse chariot races and races for fully grown horses.

The pentathlon game combined jumping, running, javelin, discus (picture ⑤) and wrestling.

▶ ⑤ Discus throwing

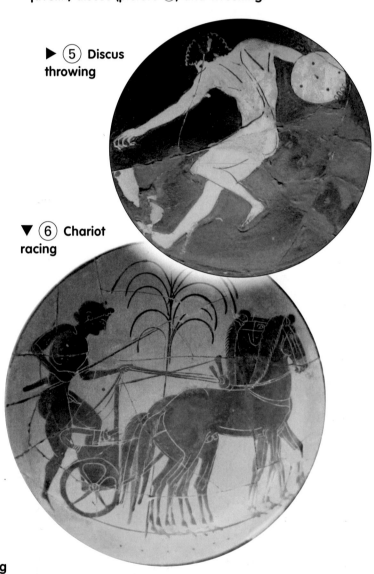

▼ ⑥ Chariot racing

◀ ⑦ Wrestling

### Day Four

The day began with a big ceremony in honour of the god Zeus and many animals were sacrificed before the games began again.

### Day Five

This was the day of the closing ceremonies, with more sacrifices and then the names and home cities of the winners of the events were read out in public. Then there was a great feast before the athletes returned to be honoured by their home cities.

Weblink: www.CurriculumVisions.com

# Glossary

**AGORA** A large open space used for a market. An agora was also a place where the citizens could discuss anything about city affairs that they wished (we now call this a forum).

**ALEXANDER THE GREAT** The most powerful ruler of the ancient Greeks and the person who, with his father, Philip, brought all of the Greeks together as a single people. He lived from 356 BC to 323 BC.

**ARCHAEN PERIOD** The archaen period (800 BC to 500 BC) represents those years when artists made larger free-standing sculptures in stiff poses with dreamlike 'archaic smiles'.

**BRONZE AGE** The time between the Stone Age and the Iron Age, when people were beginning to work with soft metals but could not get fires hot enough to extract iron from rocks. Soft metals have a limited range of uses.

**CELLA** This is actually a Roman word (from Latin for small chamber) for the inner chamber of a temple in classical architecture. It usually contained a statue of the god to whom the temple was dedicated, and a table on which offerings were placed.

**CHITON** A piece of clothing made of a single sheet and worn directly over the body, with brooches and a belt to hold it in place.

**CLASSICAL PERIOD** In this period (500 BC to 323 BC) artists perfected the style that since has been taken as the best in Greek art, with more natural-looking sculptures and buildings such as the Parthenon.

**DORIC** The Doric order was one of the types of classical architecture. The Greek Doric order was the earliest and least decorated of these, known from the 7th century BC. Its style can be seen in the columns of the Parthenon.

**FABLE** A short story or folk tale containing a moral.

**GALLEY** A ship which is partly propelled by oars. Galleys usually also had sails and used the oars only for battle, when speed and swift turns were needed.

**GREEK DARK AGES** The time after the collapse of the early civilisations that lived in Greece and the rise of the people we now call ancient Greeks. It was between about 1000 BC and 800 BC. During this time no written records were kept.

**HELLENE, HELLENISTIC PERIOD** The name we now use (Hellenic) for the Greeks. It was used in late ancient Greek times to refer to all people living in the Greek empire. Do not confuse it with Hellenistic period, which was a period from the end of the time of Alexander the Great to the Roman occupation.

**HIMATION** A kind of cloak worn over a chiton and made of a heavier material than a chiton.

**HOPLITE** The word hoplite comes from hoplon, meaning an item of armour. The armoured soldiers (hoplites) probably first appeared in the late 8th century, first as spearmen. They were mainly middle class citizens, who could afford the cost of the armour.

**IONIC** The Ionic order is one of the types of classical architecture. The Ionic order began in the mid-6th century BC in Ionia and then spread to mainland Greece in the 5th century BC. Its style is seen on buildings such as the Erechtheion.

**MYTH** A myth is a sacred story concerning the origins of the world or how the world and the creatures in it came to have their present form. The active beings in myths are generally gods and heroes.

**OLYMPIAD** A period of four years, and now connected with the Olympic Games. In ancient Greek times, an Olympiad started with the games, which were held at the beginning of the new year, which fell on the full moon closest to the summer solstice.

**OLYMPIAN** The 12 Olympians in Greek religion were the principal gods who lived on Mount Olympus. There were, at various times, 17 different gods recognised as Olympians, though never more than 12 at one time. One of the Olympians, Hades, never actually lived on the mountain, for he was the god of the underworld.

**PENINSULA** A long finger of land jutting out to sea from the mainland. Greece juts down into the Mediterranean Sea.

**PHALANX** A phalanx is a mass of heavy infantry armed with spears. The phalanx is a hallmark of ancient Greek warfare. The word phalanx comes from the Greek word phalangos, meaning finger.

**SANCTUARY** A holy area, dedicated to the gods, in which no fighting was allowed. A sanctuary could contain temples, a theatre, a gymnasium, a stadion and other features which people could enjoy together, because the ancient Greeks believed that, through athletics and plays, as well as giving tributes to the temples, they were worshipping their gods.

**TEMPLE** A holy building dedicated to a god. A temple was constructed in a sanctuary and believed to be the earthly home of the god. A colossal statue of the god was usually placed in the central room, or cella, of the temple.

**TREASURY** A building in a religious sanctuary which was a kind of strongroom in which the precious gifts were stored. City states often had their own treasuries in sanctuaries such as that in Delphi and Olympia.

**TRIREME** Ancient war galley with three rows of oars on each side.

**TYRANT** A person who has absolute power in a state or in an organisation. In ancient Greek times it simply meant anyone who overturned the government of a city state (usually through the use of popular support) to make himself a dictator.

▼ The Tholos at Delphi.

# Index